Muslim
faith and practice

Muslims at prayer.

Brian Knapp and Lisa Magloff

The Muslim faith

One must believe in certain things with mind, heart and soul; and then live by them in the course of everyday life. Faith is always personal and individual. Each person follows the faith they choose. Here are some main parts of the Muslim faith.

Islamic beliefs:

▶ There is only one supreme and eternal God, Allah, who is all-knowing and the final judge of people.

▶ God appointed messengers, called prophets, to deliver divine messages. Mohammed (pbuh) was the final messenger of God.

▶ Muslims should follow the five pillars of Islam: professing faith by acknowledging "There is no God but Allah, Mohammed is His Prophet"; daily prayer; charity through alms giving; fasting during the month of Ramadan; pilgrimage to Mecca.

▶ The Qur'an is the word of God. It was given to the prophet Mohammed (pbuh) by the angel Gabriel.

▶ Each person communicates directly with God, everyone is equal in the eyes of God.

▶ There will be a Day of Judgement when all men and women from Adam to the last person, will be resurrected for judgement. On that day, the good will be rewarded and welcomed in Heaven while the bad will be punished and cast into Hell.

▶ A Muslim should always be truthful and should follow the laws of Islam.

▶ Salvation can only be obtained through God's Grace and not through a person's efforts, yet everyone should do good and avoid all sins. Total submission to the will of God is the single path to salvation.

▶ The good Muslim surrenders all pride, the chief among sins, and follows explicitly the will of Allah as revealed in the Qur'an.

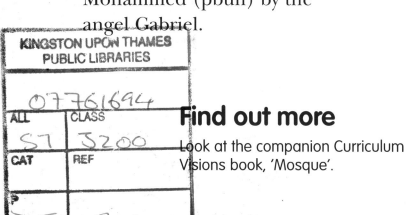
Find out more

Look at the companion Curriculum Visions book, 'Mosque'.

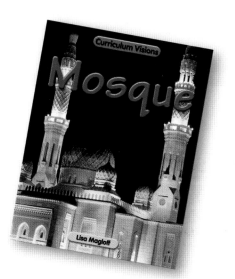

Curriculum Visions

Mosque

Lisa Magloff

Contents

As you go through the book, look for words in **BOLD CAPITALS**. These words are defined in the glossary.

In this book you will see the letters (pbuh) after the name Mohammed. They mean 'praise be unto him' and are a sign of respect.

 Understanding others

Remember that other people's beliefs are important to them. You must always be considerate and understanding when studying about faith.

A Muslim boy in traditional clothing.

What it means to be a Muslim

A Muslim is a person who believes that there is one God (Allah) and that Mohammed (pbuh) was His prophet.

ISLAM is one of the world's great faiths, and is practised by one in five of the world's people. The word Islam is an ARABIC word which means peace and 'submission to the will of God'. A person who practises Islam is called a MUSLIM, which means 'a person who surrenders to the will of God'.

Beliefs

Islam is not exactly the same all over the world, but there are six basic beliefs that most Muslims share: There is only one God; Mohammed (PBUH) was God's final PROPHET; the QUR'AN is the word of God and contains God's final message; God also created angels; there will be a resurrection and a Day of Judgement, when the dead will rise up to be judged by God and sent to either HEAVEN or HELL; everything that happens, happens only by the will of God.

Allah, the One and Only God

The core of the Islamic faith is that there is only one God. The Arabic word for God is ALLAH. Allah represents everyone on Earth – even those who do not believe in God.

Mohammed

MOHAMMED (pbuh) was born in Mecca, in modern Saudi Arabia, in 570 CE. He was chosen by God to hear and teach God's message.

Muslims believe that God sent many prophets and gave humans many messages throughout history. The prophets include Adam, Abraham, Moses, David and Jesus. But Mohammed (pbuh) was God's final prophet and the message that he brought was God's final and thus most important message.

The Qur'an

Muslims believe that the Qur'an is the final message of God. It was given to Mohammed (pbuh) and contains the exact words of God.

◀ Praying to Allah is a daily part of the Muslim faith.

Angels

Islam also includes the belief in a spirit world, created by God, which we cannot see. The world includes ANGELS (mala'ika in Arabic) who are the winged messengers of Allah.

Day of judgement (Qiyamah)

The Qur'an teaches that, at some time in the future, the bodies and souls of the dead will be reunited, the book that records each person's life will be opened, and each person's deeds will be judged by God. Souls that are found worthy will be sent to Heaven and those found unworthy will be sent to Hell.

▲ Muslims go to the MOSQUE to worship, and also to learn more about the principles of Islam. These people are learning about the principles and beliefs of Islam during a talk at a mosque.

Fate

Islam teaches that everything happens by the will of God. Whatever happens in this world happens according to God's decision and plan. This principle is known as "the decision and determination of Allah" (in Arabic, al-qada' wa al-qadar). At the same time, everyone is free to make their own decisions. Since we cannot know what God's plan is for us, we must make the best decisions we can.

A Muslim way of life

For many, Islam is a way of life, not only a way of worshipping.

The Qur'an tells Muslims that people are Allah's assistants on Earth and are responsible for taking care of everything from the environment to the people around us. The Qur'an tells Muslims that it is important to live in a way which emphasises justice, kindness and the avoidance of wrongdoing. We can see from this that faith affects almost every aspect of everyday life for Muslims.

Islamic Law

Muslims believe that God, through Mohammed (pbuh), gave certain laws to people. These are ways of living in accordance with God's wishes. The **FIVE PILLARS OF ISLAM** are the most important laws in the Qur'an, but there are many more.

For example, **ISLAMIC LAW** does not allow Muslims to eat animals that have died from natural causes. To be eaten, an animal must have its throat cut with a clean knife and its head facing **MECCA**, and a special prayer must be said after the animal is killed. Animals that are killed like this are called lawful, or **HALAL**. Most Muslims only eat meat that is halal. But foods other than meat are always fine to eat.

Daily prayer

The Qur'an says that Muslims should try to pray at five given times throughout the day. The prayers can be said anywhere, so many Muslims say their daily prayers in a quiet place at school or work and make them a regular part of their everyday life.

◀ Food which is prepared according to the Qur'an is called halal.

▲ Many Muslim women cover their heads. This is also a part of Islamic law. But the way that they cover their head is up to the tradition and custom of the place where they are from.

▶ Learning is very important in Islam. Muslims are encouraged to learn Arabic so they can read the Qur'an in its original language.

Learning

Learning has always played a huge part in Islam. This is partly because of the desire of every Muslim to be able to read the Qur'an and other writings in the original Arabic. Today, learning to read and write Arabic, and to recite the Qur'an, is very important and many people attend special schools at mosques to learn this. But all types of learning and education are valued very highly by Muslims.

Community of faith

Islam teaches that all Muslims belong to a worldwide community of believers, called the UMMAH. Every Muslim is a part of this community and can turn to it for assistance and companionship in faith.

◀ Community is the cornerstone of Islam. Every Muslim belongs to the worldwide community of Muslims. Muslims from around the world support and help each other.

Weblink: www.CurriculumVisions.com

Mohammed the prophet (pbuh)

Mohammed (pbuh) was the last of the prophets sent to Earth by Allah.

The prophet **MOHAMMED** (pbuh) was born in 570 CE in modern day Saudi Arabia. The name Mohammed (pbuh) means 'highly praised'. *map →*

Mohammed's early life

Mohammed's parents died when he was very young, and he was brought up near Mecca by his grandfather and then by his uncle.

As a boy, Mohammed (pbuh) worked hard, tending sheep for his family and later becoming a trader and caravan leader.

When he was 25 years old, a rich widow named Khadijah hired him to work as a trader. The two fell in love and were married soon after. They had six children, four girls and two boys, but not all of them survived to adulthood.

At this time, the people of Mecca worshipped many gods and **IDOLS**. All of these were kept in a building called the **KA'BA** in Mecca, which was believed to be the site of the first place of worship on Earth, built by Adam.

When Mohammed (pbuh) was about 35, the Ka'ba caught fire and burnt. Everyone in Mecca helped to rebuild it. When it came to replacing the sacred black stone inside of the Ka'ba no one could agree who should have the honour.

Mohammed (pbuh) placed the stone on a clean cloth, got all of the leaders to lift it together and then he placed the stone in the Ka'ba.

From this time onward, Mohammed (pbuh) became greatly concerned about the way that the people of Mecca worshipped many gods instead of one God.

The revelations begin

Mohammed (pbuh) would often go into the desert, to a cave on Mount Hira, and think about the nature of God. In 610 CE, when Mohammed (pbuh) was 40, the angel Gabriel came to visit him in the cave, and announced that Mohammed (pbuh) had been chosen as God's messenger.

At first Mohammed (pbuh) preached among his friends, but later he preached more openly and in front of more and more people.

The emigration

The leaders of Mecca became very angry with Mohammed (pbuh), as they did not want to give up their gods. In 622, Mohammed (pbuh) and his followers were forced to flee Mecca to the city of **MEDINA**, 250 miles away.

This escape to Medina is called the flight or **EMIGRATION** (hijirah in Arabic) and it is the date on which the Muslim calendar starts.

In Medina, people were familiar with the idea of one God and after just a few years, most of them had converted to Islam.

In 628, the leaders of Mecca raised an army to fight Mohammed (pbuh), but he was able to defeat them. Mohammed (pbuh) returned to Mecca that year and from this time on he was accepted by the people as the true prophet of God.

By 632, Islam had spread around the Arabian peninsula. In that year, Mohammed (pbuh) made a special trip to the Ka'ba in Mecca. On a nearby hill he preached his last sermon. Mohammed (pbuh) died on June 8, 632.

The meaning of the prophet's life

Muslims believe that Mohammed (pbuh) had to struggle and suffer many times, just as we all do in our lives. For example, he suffered when he was kicked out of Mecca. Mohammed's (pbuh) life, therefore, was a demonstration of the battle between good and evil, truth and falsehood, justice and oppression.

The prophet Mohammed's (pbuh) suffering is also a reminder that everyone can be either good or bad, and that we have to struggle in order to overcome evil and be good people.

As a result, Muslims believe that one of the best ways to overcome evil is to love the prophet Mohammed (pbuh) and follow his teachings and his example in how we live our lives.

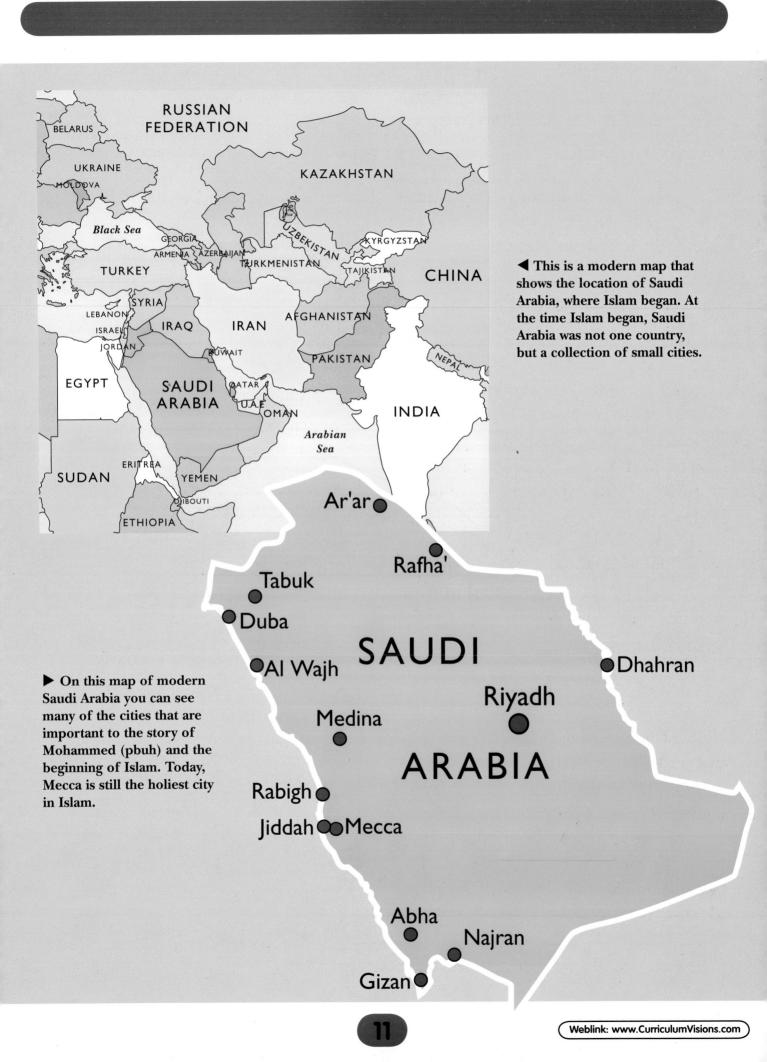

◀ This is a modern map that shows the location of Saudi Arabia, where Islam began. At the time Islam began, Saudi Arabia was not one country, but a collection of small cities.

▶ On this map of modern Saudi Arabia you can see many of the cities that are important to the story of Mohammed (pbuh) and the beginning of Islam. Today, Mecca is still the holiest city in Islam.

11

Holy scriptures

The Qur'an is the word of Allah. It was revealed to the prophet Mohammed (pbuh).

The basis of the Islamic faith is the holy **QUR'AN**, the word of God. God sent the angel Gabriel to the prophet Mohammed (pbuh) to give the Qur'an to him. This was done little-by-little over a period of 23 years.

Mohammed (pbuh) memorised the holy words and recited the messages to his followers, who also memorised them.

The history of the Qur'an

The Qur'an consists of 114 chapters, known as **SURAHS**. Each surah is made up of a number of verses and is a different length. As Mohammed (pbuh) recited each surah to his followers, he also told them which surahs went before and after it, so that they could be put together in the order that God intended.

▼ The Qur'an is the holy book of Islam.

The first written copy of the entire Qur'an was made just after Mohammed's (pbuh) death. All other copies of the Qur'an are copied from this original.

God sent the Qur'an to Mohammed (pbuh) in Arabic, so the Qur'an is written in that language. Although the Qur'an has been translated into most languages, Muslims all over the world also try to learn Arabic so that they may be able to read the Qur'an in its original language. The reason for this is that, when you translate a language, some of the meaning may be lost. As the Qur'an is the word of God, nothing should be lost by translating it.

What is in the Qur'an?

The first parts of the Qur'an given to Mohammed (pbuh) set the foundation for the faith. Some of these early surahs talk about God and faith, while others discuss more practical matters, such as what kind of food can be eaten. Later surahs discuss Islam in more detail.

Memorising the Qur'an

Because the Qur'an is the word of God, both the messages in the Qur'an and the words themselves are holy. Mohammed's (pbuh) early followers memorised all of the Qur'an, and learning parts of the Qur'an by heart is a part of worship for all Muslims.

All Muslims have the first surah (called the **FATIHAH**) memorised because it is part of the daily prayers. It provides a simple guide to the most basic desire of Muslims, namely, to follow Allah's will:

In the name of God, Most Gracious, Most Merciful.

All praises are for Allah who is Lord of the world;

He is the most kind and most merciful.

He is the king of the Day of Judgement.

We worship you alone and ask you for help.

Show us the correct path, the path of people whom you have blessed, not on whom your anger is upon nor the people who have been led astray.

▼ Learning parts of the Qur'an by heart is an important part of Islamic religious education.

A Muslim who has learned the entire Qur'an by heart is given the title of HAFIZ. Very few people manage to do this, so anyone with the title hafiz is treated with great respect.

Islamic Law

The main source of teachings in Islam is the Qur'an. But Muslims also believe that the sayings and actions of Mohammed (pbuh) are very important, because they are an interpretation of the will of Allah. The Qur'an says: "Obey Allah and obey the Messenger."

The actual sayings and deeds of the prophet Mohammed (pbuh) are called SUNNAH. Mohammed's (pbuh) early followers also wrote down what they could remember about his life and these writings are called the SEERAH. Together, these are called the HADITH.

The need for the Hadith

The Qur'an paints what must be done with a broad brush. It does not go into the detail needed for everyday life. This was part of Mohammed's (pbuh) role as prophet. So, for example, the Qur'an commands people to pray, but it was Mohammed (pbuh) who showed people exactly how to pray by saying "Pray as you see me praying." So, Muslims learned to pray by following Mohammed's (pbuh) actions.

Shari'ah

The Qur'an and the Hadith, together with the interpretations of the Hadith made by scholars over the centuries, are called ISLAMIC LAW (SHARI'AH).

In Islam there is no difference between religion and everyday life. Muslims therefore look to the Shari'ah (pronounced *sha-ree-ah*) to help them with everyday life and to know what is right, and how to behave according to God's will, in different circumstances.

Muslims always follow the laws of the country they are in, but where they can, they also follow Islamic Law. This brings special responsibilities.

▼ An IMAM discusses Islamic Law and belief in a mosque.

Some Islamic laws

To a Muslim, a sin is something which offends God. If a Muslim commits a sin, they not only offend God, but bring disgrace on other Muslims, too.

Muslims know that you cannot avoid slipping up and making mistakes occasionally, but if you continue to do wrong, you are showing contempt for Islam and for God.

Keeping your honour

Muslims believe that every person is loved by God. So, any time you harm others you also harm yourself. Stealing, for example, is forbidden, because it injures others, and brings shame on yourself, your family and your faith.

Keeping clean

To be clean, you have to be clean both on the outside and inside. This is why Muslims wash before going to prayer. But to stay clean on the inside, Muslims must not have alcohol or drugs, or eat any animal that was not killed in a certain way (halal).

All people are equal

In Islam, race and ethnic origin are unimportant. Men and women are equal. Thus anyone treating women, or people of another race or religion, disrespectfully brings shame on themself and on Islam.

The five pillars of Islam

There are five fundamental requirements of Islam, called the five pillars of Islam.

First pillar: Shahada

The Muslim profession of faith is called the **SHAHADA**, which means 'bearing witness'. This is said out loud before and during each of the five daily prayers. It is whispered into a baby's ear at birth, and at the time of death. In Arabic, it is:

La ilaha illal lah Mohammed ar rasul lallah (There is no God but Allah, and Mohammed is the prophet of Allah).

Second pillar: Daily prayer

Prayer is the heart of the Muslim faith. Many children begin saying prayers at age seven. Muslims pray to show obedience to God, and to ask God for guidance in daily life. The Arabic word for prayer is **SALAH**.

Prayer occurs five times a day: before sunrise, at noon, in mid-afternoon, immediately after sunset, and before midnight or going to bed. Muslims can either pray together at a mosque, or on their own, wherever they are. Prayers must be said while facing towards Mecca.

Preparing for prayer

Before praying, Muslims remove their shoes and go through a routine washing ritual, cleansing themselves in preparation for prayer. The ritual washing, called **WUDU**, can be done in any clean place where there is water. There are special rules to allow for situations when water is not available (for example, in a desert).

◀ Remove your shoes.

▲ Wash both hands up to the wrists. Do this three times

3

▲ Rinse the mouth with water using the right hand. Do this three times.

4

▲ Wash the nostrils by sniffing up water and blowing it out. You perform this three times.

5

▲ Wash the face three times.

6

7

▲ Wash each arm up to the elbow. Do this three times.

◀ Wipe or rub the head with the fingers. Do this once.

▼ Wash the feet up to the ankles. Do this three times.

10

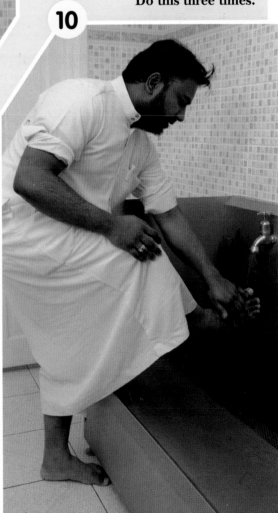

8

▲ Clean the inside of the ears with the index fingers and the back of the ears with the thumbs. Do this once.

9

▲ Wipe the back of the neck. Do this once.

Salah (prayer)

The sequence of daily prayers is called SALAH. Salah is a time to re-dedicate yourself to Allah. The movements of the prayer help you to make contact with God. The set of movements is shown here. One complete set of movements is called a RAK'AH. During prayers, the rak'ah is repeated two, three or four times – the exact number depends on which of the five daily prayers is being performed.

▼ Put your left hand on your chest and your right hand over it and say quietly: "Glory and praise to you, O God; blessed is your name and exalted is your majesty. There is no God other than you. I come seeking shelter from Satan, the condemned one." Now recite the opening chapter of the Qur'an. After this you may recite any other passage from the Qur'an.

▼ TAKBIR. Shut out everything and concentrate on God. Do this by facing Mecca and making a clear intention to pray for God as God has commanded.

▼ Begin the rak'ah. Stand straight up with your hands by your ears and say "Allahu Akbar" (God is Supreme).

1

2

3

4

◀ RUKU. Bow by bending forwards with your hands on your knees while keeping the back straight. While doing this, say "Glory be to God the great, and praise to him." Repeat this three times.

6

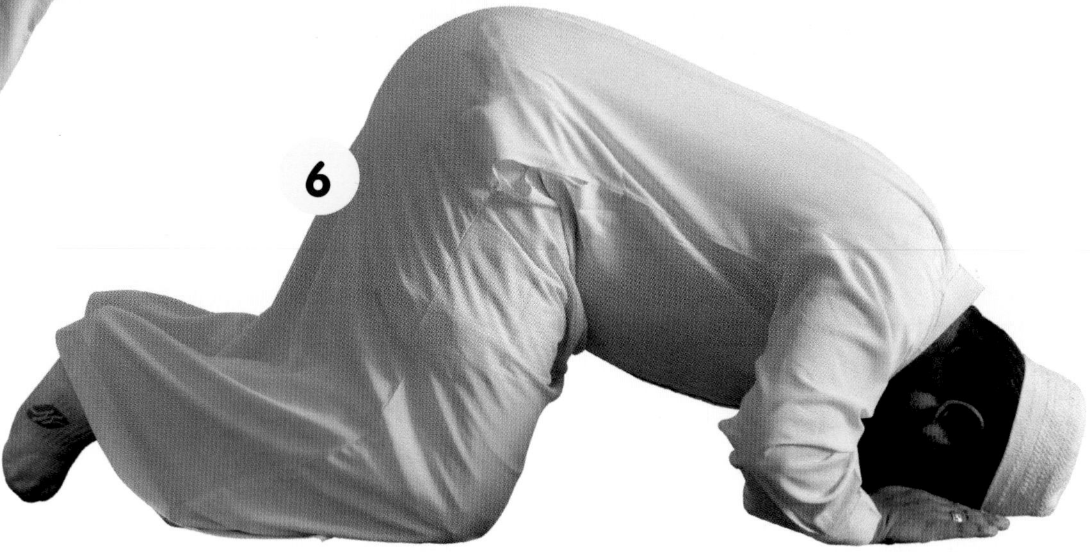

▲ SUJUD. Prostrate yourself by kneeling, with your forehead, nose, hands, knees and toes all on the ground. Say, "Glory be to my Lord, the Most High. Allah is greater than everything else." Repeat this three times.

▼ SALAM (peace). Look right and then left and then say, "Peace be with you and the mercy of Allah.

5

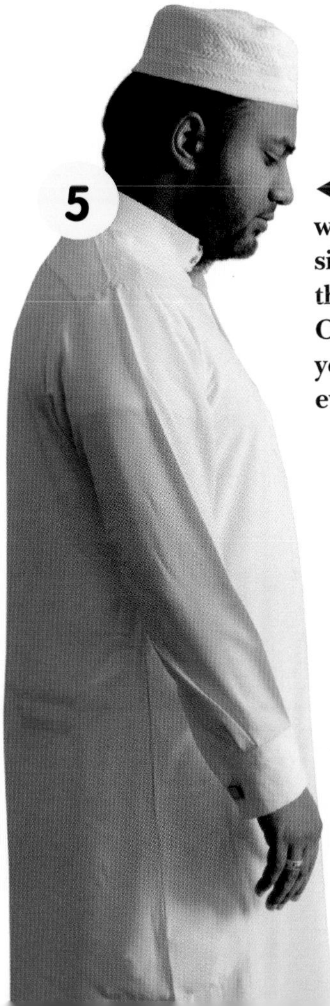

◀ QUIYAM. Stand up with your hands by your sides and say, "God hears those who praise him. Oh God, all praise be to you, O God greater than everything else."

7

▶ JULUS. Rise to a kneeling position with your hands on your knees and say a short, silent prayer. Then repeat sujud. Then say a short prayer for the community of Muslims and for your sins to be forgiven.

Friday prayers (Yawm-al-jumu'ah)

Friday is the day of congregational worship, that is the time when all Muslims meet and pray together at a mosque or other place (such as a large room which has been prepared by laying down clean sheets). The JUM'AH (Friday) congregational prayer is held in the early afternoon.

Third pillar: Almsgiving (zakah)

The Qur'an teaches that wealth and money should be used to help Islam. Every Muslim who can afford it should give up part of their money every year to help others. This is called ZAKAH. The word zakah means to purify, or to make clean.

Who pays zakah

Only people who can afford it have to pay zakah. Zakah is not paid out of duty or law, but out of belief in Islam.

The amount that should be paid is usually one-fortieth (2.5%) of all the money, land, property and jewellery that a person has. The money can be given to mosques, schools or organisations that help the poor.

Charity is different from zakah. Many Muslims also give to charity, in addition to zakah. Zakah is a certain amount that should be paid each year, but the amount given to charity is up to each person to decide.

Fourth pillar: Fasting (sawm)

Mohammed (pbuh) received the first verses of the Qur'an during the month of Ramadan (the ninth month of the Islamic calendar) and so this month has a special significance.

Every day during Ramadan, Muslims fast from dawn to sunset, in remembrance of Allah's gift of the Qur'an. The period of fasting

is set out in the Qur'an:

> "O You who believe! Fasting is prescribed for you, even as it was prescribed for those before you, that you may attain God-consciousness."

Most older children and all adults observe the fast, except those who are ill or travelling, or women who are pregnant or nursing. These people can make up the fast later.

During Ramadan, everyone gets up before dawn and eats a big meal, called SOHAR. Nothing else will be eaten or drunk until sunset. As soon as the Sun sets, the fast can be broken, traditionally by eating a few dates and drinking water. This is followed by prayer, and then a proper meal, called IFTAR, is eaten.

Ramadan is more than a time of not eating, it is a time to reflect on the teachings in the Qur'an and on God.

Taraweeh

During Ramadan there is a special night-time prayer session called TARAWEEH. Traditionally, a person who has memorised the whole Qur'an recites it, in small portions and in the correct order, every night, completing the recitation of the entire Qur'an just before the end of the month of Ramadan.

Seclusion

The prophet Mohammed (pbuh) spent the last ten days and nights of Ramadan praying in seclusion. To keep up this tradition, some people spend the last ten days of Ramadan praying in the mosque.

The day of Eid

This festival marks the end of Ramadan. You will find information about it on pages 28–29.

Fifth pillar: Pilgrimage (Hajj)

The final pillar of Islam is the pilgrimage (**HAJJ**) to Mecca during the twelfth month of the Islamic calendar, called Dhu al-Hijjah. Every Muslim aims to perform this at least once in their life.

The Hajj involves a visit to Mecca (see diagram on pages 24–25). Once there, a series of rites are performed over several days at the Ka'ba and in the nearby areas of Mina, Muzdalifah and Arafat. Each of these places has a special significance for Muslims. A shorter pilgrimage, called umrah, forms part of the Hajj, but may be performed by itself at any time.

Ihram

Before leaving for the Hajj, pilgrims must be in a special state of holiness and purity, called **IHRAM**. This is achieved by washing and declaring their intention, through prayer, to make the pilgrimage for God.

Once they have declared their intention, men put on two large pieces of seamless, unstitched white cloth that symbolises the purity of ihram. Women wear a similar garment made of three pieces of cloth. Most pilgrims will wear only these clothes and a pair of sandals throughout their pilgrimage.

▼ During the Hajj, millions of pilgrims come to the Ka'ba in Mecca. The Ka'ba is the square building covered with a black cloth. It is in the middle of a larger mosque. In this photo, you can see thousands of pilgrims circling the Ka'ba.

The Ka'ba

The Hajj begins at the Ka'ba in Mecca. The Ka'ba is a cube-shaped, brick building, about 15 m high, in the centre of the mosque called the Masjid al-Haram (Great Mosque). The Ka'ba is covered with a black silk cloth embroidered with gold lettering. Inside the Ka'ba is a sacred black stone, the Hajar al-Aswad.

The Ka'ba was originally built by Adam, the first human, as the first place to worship God. After Adam finished building the Ka'ba, God gave him a white stone to put inside. When people touched the stone as they worshipped, the stone absorbed their sins and began to turn black. This is the black stone inside the Ka'ba today. Later, the Ka'ba was rebuilt by the prophet Abraham.

23

Over the centuries, the Ka'ba was destroyed and rebuilt several times, and in Mohammed's (pbuh) time it had become a shrine to **PAGAN** gods. Mohammed (pbuh) re-dedicated it as a house of God.

Upon their arrival in Mecca, pilgrims enter the Great Mosque and perform umrah – they circle seven times around the outside of the Ka'ba. After this, pilgrims pray at the Station of Abraham and drink from a spring, called the zamzam, which runs through the Great Mosque. Pilgrims then walk seven times between the nearby hills of Safa and Marwah.

According to Muslim tradition, Ishmail, the son of Abraham, and his mother Hagar, were wandering between these hills and dying of thirst, when God caused a spring to start flowing. The water came out so fast that Hagar shouted "Zam! Zam!", which means "Stop! Stop!" in Arabic.

Arafat and Mina

After performing umrah, pilgrims leave Mecca and travel to the nearby valley of Mina. On the next day, they leave before dawn for the plain of Arafat, where they perform

▼ The stages of the Hajj.

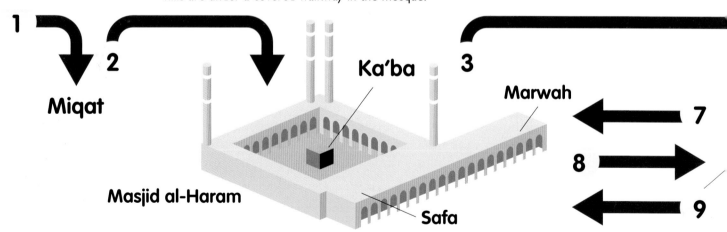

(1) Before the eighth day of Dhu al-Hijjah, pilgrims bathe, change into special clothes and declare their intention to make the pilgrimage for God.

(2) On the eighth day of Dhu al-Hijjah, the pilgrims enter Mecca and go to the Great Mosque and perform tawaf-circling seven times around the Ka'ba without stopping, while reciting prayers. Then the pilgrims perform sa'ee – they walk seven times between the hills of Safa and Marwah. The hills are under a covered walkway in the mosque.

(3) In the evening of the eighth day of Dhu al-Hijjah the pilgrims travel about six kilometres to Mina and say prayers. Pilgrims spend the night in Mina and leave after sunrise on the ninth day of Dhu al-Hijjah.

1

2

Miqat

Ka'ba

3

Marwah

7

8

9

Masjid al-Haram

Safa

(9) After leaving Mina in the evening of the twelfth or thirteenth day of Dhu al-Hijjah, the pilgrims return to Mecca to perform a farewell tawaf and farewell prayers.

(7) and (8) The pilgrims then return to Mecca for another tawaf (circling the Ka'ba) and sa'ee (walking between Safa and Marwah). Pilgrims may also pray at the shrine of Abraham and drink from the zamzam. The pilgrims then return to Mina for the night. Beginning on the tenth of Dhu al-Hijjah is the Muslim holiday of Eid al-Adha. Pilgrims celebrate this in Mina.

On the eleventh and twelfth days of Dhu al-Hijjah the pilgrims stay in Mina and stone the Jumat pillars each day. The pilgrims can leave Mina on the twelfth day, or they may stay another day.

'the standing'. This is the central rite of the Hajj. Here pilgrims pray for forgiveness as a reminder of the Day of Judgement.

It was at Arafat, on the Mount of Mercy, that Mohammed delivered his last sermon, asking God to pardon the sins of pilgrims who stood at Arafat.

At Arafat, Muslims feel the presence and closeness of a merciful God. This is why the pilgrims leave Arafat joyfully, feeling reborn and without sin.

On their way back to Mina the pilgrims stop at Muzdalifah to rest, pray and gather small stones. Once back in Mina, pilgrims throw seven pebbles at each of three stone pillars. The pillars represent Satan. In Mina, pilgrims also sacrifice an animal. This is a reminder of the time God asked Abraham to prove his faith by sacrificing his son. Abraham agreed, but at the last moment, God told Abraham to sacrifice a sheep instead.

After this, pilgrims return to Mecca and again walk seven times around the Ka'ba. Men shave or cut their hair (and shave their beards) and women trim their hair. This is the end of the Hajj.

All throughout the Hajj, pilgrims recite a prayer called Talbiya: "Here I am, Oh God, at Your command! Here I am at Your command! You are without associate! Here I am at Your command! To You are all praise, grace and dominion! You are without associate!"

(4) Pilgrims arrive in Arafat, about three kilometres from Mina, on the ninth day of Dhu al-Hijjah. Special prayers are said on entering Arafat. Pilgrims can stay anywhere in Arafat or on the Mount of Mercy. Pilgrims stay here until sunset, reciting prayers, reading the Qur'an and asking God for forgiveness.

(5) After sunset on the ninth day of Dhu al-Hijjah the pilgrims leave Arafat for Muzdalifah, about three kilometres away. Here, pilgrims spend the night. While in Muzdalifah, each pilgrim collects small stones.

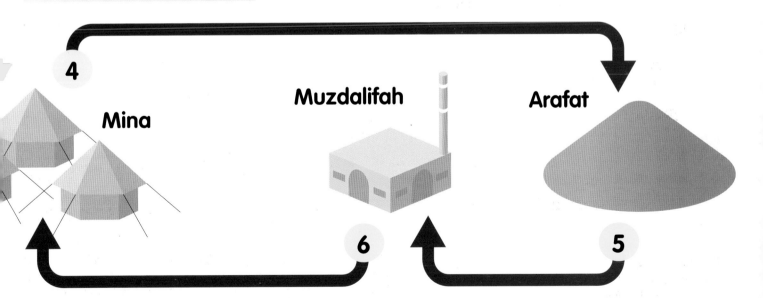

Mina Muzdalifah Arafat

(6) Before sunrise on the tenth day of Dhu al-Hijjah, the pilgrims go back to Mina. At Mina, pilgrims throw their stones at three pillars (Jumarat pillars), which represent Satan. Each pilgrim then buys and sacrifices an animal. After this pilgrims shave and cut their hair and can change into normal clothes.

Symbols of Islam

There are many symbols used in Islam, but pictures of people are never used.

Muslims believe that it is wrong to worship idols. They avoid having images or paintings of the prophets or of God, so there can be no mistake that the image is being worshipped. But there are some symbols that have a special meaning for Muslims.

Words and art

For Muslims, the words given by God to Mohammed (pbuh) are holy in themselves. So, creating art which uses words is an important way of showing how much those words mean. A great deal of Islamic art is made by using **CALLIGRAPHY** to make God's word look beautiful.

Crescent Moon

You may have seen a Crescent Moon on flags of Islamic countries, or on Muslim buildings. The Crescent Moon is a reminder that all life comes and goes, just like the phases of the Moon.

The Crescent Moon also shows Muslims how Islam guides and lights their way through life, just like the Moon guided the first Muslims through the deserts of Arabia.

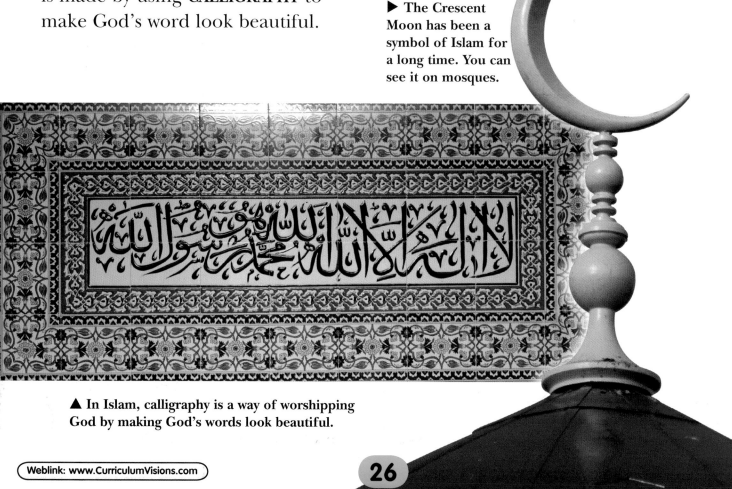

▶ The Crescent Moon has been a symbol of Islam for a long time. You can see it on mosques.

▲ In Islam, calligraphy is a way of worshipping God by making God's words look beautiful.

Skullcap

Many Muslims believe that they should keep their heads covered when they pray, out of respect. Some Muslim men wear a small cap called a skullcap, prayer cap, kufi or tigyha, while they are at prayer. The cap is usually made from white, crocheted cotton.

▼▶ A skullcap can be any colour, but white is the most common.

Prayer beads (subha)

According to Islamic tradition, the prophet Mohammed (pbuh) said, "To God belongs 99 names, 100 minus 1, anyone who memorises them will enter Paradise; He (Allah) is odd (since there is only one God), and He loves odd numbers." So, many Muslims believe that repeating the 99 different Islamic names of God over and over brings them closer to God. Prayer beads are used to keep track of how many names have been recited. The beads usually have three sets of 33 small beads and one large bead.

The first six names of God are: Allah; Ar-Rahman, the Most Compassionate, the Beneficent, the Gracious; Ar-Rahim, the Merciful; Al-Malik, the King, the Monarch; Al-Quddus, the Most Holy; As-Salam, the All-Peaceful, the Bestower of peace.

The colour green

Many mosques and Islamic buildings are painted green. Green is said to have been Mohammed's (pbuh) favourite colour. Islam began in the desert, where there were few plants, and so green also reminds Muslims of the paradise that waits for them in Heaven.

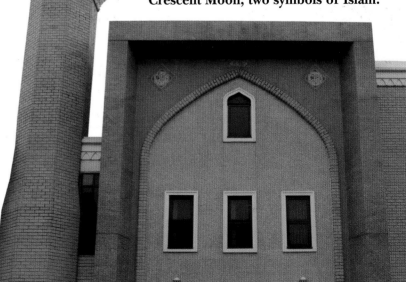

▼ This mosque has green tiles and a Crescent Moon, two symbols of Islam.

Weblink: www.CurriculumVisions.com

Islamic celebrations

There are two Muslim festivals that all Muslims celebrate: Eid al-Fitr and Eid al-Adha. But there are many other chances for celebration, too.

The Arabic word for festival is **EID**. Muslims see celebration and festivals as a way of thanking Allah.

The dates and days of celebration are set according to the Islamic calendar. The Islamic calendar is based on the phases of the Moon. Each month starts when the Moon is new, and ends when the next New Moon comes around.

There are 12 months in this calendar, and each month has either 29 or 30 days, depending on when the Moon is new. There is no leap year. This means that the Islamic calendar is 11 days shorter than the western calendar. Because of this, Muslim holidays happen 11 days earlier each year. So all the holidays move through the seasons over the years.

There are two Eids set down by the Qur'an. These are holy days. There is a big difference between ordinary days for celebration and holy days. Muslims celebrate national holidays just the same as anyone else. But, of course, holidays have no religious significance.

▲ On the Eids, Muslims go to mosque for special prayers. Many people wear traditional clothing.

month following Ramadan and marks the end of Ramadan, the month of fasting. It is a public holiday in Islamic countries and everyone celebrates.

People gather together and join in Eid prayers, exchange sweets and give gifts to children. Muslims who can afford it are asked to give Sadaqat al-Fitr, a form of charity for the poor.

Eid al-Fitr

EID AL-FITR holy day occurs on 1 Shawwal (the tenth month in the Islamic calendar), the first day of the

Eid al-Adha

EID AL-ADHA (the Feast of the Sacrifice) happens on the tenth day of the twelfth month (the month of

▼ After prayer, it is time to eat a celebratory meal.

the pilgrimage, Dhu al-Hijjah) in the Islamic calendar. It is two months and ten days after Eid al-Fitr and marks the end of the season of pilgrimage, or Hajj.

The Feast of the Sacrifice celebrates an event that happened in biblical times. God told the prophet Abraham to prove his faith and obedience to God by killing, or sacrificing, his son Ishmael. Abraham prepared to do it, but God stopped him just in time, and told Abraham to sacrifice a sheep instead.

In order to celebrate Abraham's obedience to God, and God's mercy in allowing Ishmael

to live, each Muslim family also sacrifices an animal on the Feast of the Sacrifice. The animal sacrificed is usually a sheep, a cow, a goat or even a camel. The sacrifice is conducted by a halal butcher. The meat is then cut up into three parts: one-third is given to the poor, one-third to relatives and friends, and one-third is eaten by the family.

After the sacrifice, Muslims go to the mosque for prayers, and then have a big feast.

Other festivals

There are many other Muslim festivals throughout the world. For example, the birthday of Mohammed (pbuh) and of Muslim saints are not Islamic holidays, but some people celebrate them with a type of festival called a **MAWLID**. A mawlid may involve a local carnival or a party. Other Muslim festivals are local celebrations that take place in just one country or region. For example, the end of Ramadan is celebrated in Nigeria with the sallah festival.

◀ At the Eid, people greet each other by embracing and wishing each other a happy Eid with the words "Eid mubarak".

Glossary

ALLAH The Arabic word for God, the Creator of the universe.

ANGELS Beings created by God to praise and obey God.

ARABIC The language spoken by Mohammed (pbuh), and so the language the Qur'an was written in. Not all Muslims speak Arabic, but many try to learn it.

CALLIGRAPHY A type of writing where the words are made to be beautiful to look at as well as to read.

CE This abbreviation stands for 'common era'. This is another way of writing AD (which is a translation of the Latin words *anno domini*, or 'after the death of our Lord') when writing dates.

EID Islamic religious holidays and occasions for celebration.

EID AL-ADHA (Feast of the Sacrifice) The second of two main religious festivals in Islam. The festival commemorates the day on which the prophet Abraham tried to fulfil Allah's command to sacrifice his son, but was prevented from doing so by an angel. The festival lasts for four days and is a time of feasting, rejoicing and remembrance.

EID AL-FITR The first of the two major festivals in Islam. It is also known as the 'Festival of the breaking of the fast'. It marks the end of the month of fasting (Ramadan) and is a time of great joy.

EMIGRATION (HIJIRAH) The time, in 622, when Mohammed (pbuh) and his followers were forced to flee Mecca and go to Medina.

FATIHAH The first verse (surah) of the Qur'an.

FIVE PILLARS OF ISLAM The five main values and practices of Islam. They are: the shahada, prayer, almsgiving, fasting during Ramadan and the Hajj.

HADITH This word literally means 'sayings'. It is the title given to the collection of recorded words and actions of the prophet Mohammed (pbuh) which serve as an explanation of the meaning of the Holy Qur'an.

HAFIZ The title given to a person who has memorised the entire Qur'an.

HAJJ The fifth of the five pillars of Islam. It involves a pilgrimage to Mecca to worship at the Kaba and to re-dedicate themselves to Allah at sites important in his life. The Hajj is immediately followed by the festival of Eid al-Adha.

HALAL Something lawful or permitted in Islam. This word usually refers to animals which have been killed in an approved way, or are lawful to eat. For example, the Qur'an says not to eat pork, so pork is not halal and cannot be eaten by Muslims.

HEAVEN (JANNAH OR PARADISE) The place where those who achieve salvation will live after death. The word jannah means 'garden' in Arabic.

HELL Only Allah knows the true nature of Heaven and Hell, but in the Qur'an they are described in human terms so we can understand them. Hell is described as a terrible place full of suffering.

IDOL An image (statue or painting) that people worship.

IFTAR Every day during Ramadan, the fast is broken at sunset with a meal called iftar.

IHRAM The state of being ready to make the Hajj. This involves being physically ready as well as being mentally and spiritually ready.

IMAM Imam is a religious scholar or someone very knowledgeable about Islam who leads the congregational prayers.

ISLAM The religion followed by Muslims. The word Islam means 'Submission to God'.

ISLAMIC LAW (SHARI'AH) The term 'Shari'ah' means all the elements of a proper Islamic life; these include proper moral behaviour, proper respect towards Allah, correct belief, proper personal piety, and so on. In other words, it means the right way to live one's life as a Muslim.

JULUS One of the positions used during daily prayer. It is a sitting position. A person sits on their left leg and foot. The left foot is resting on its back, the right foot is resting on the inside toes. Arms and hands rest on the thighs, fingers straight and slightly apart.

JUM'AH The group (congregational) prayers that take place on Fridays in the mosque.

KA'BA The cubed looking structure in Mecca towards which all Muslims pray. This is the first house of worship built by Adam and rebuilt by Abraham.

MAWLID A festival, usually in honour of the birthday of Mohammed (pbuh) or another important Muslim.

MECCA The sacred city of Islam, located in modern Saudia Arabia. Mecca is the home of the Ka'ba and is where Muslims perform their pilgrimage during Hajj.

MEDINA The city which was the first political centre of Islam. Mohammed's (pbuh) grave site and mosque are located in this city.

MOHAMMED (pbuh) The founder of Islam. To Muslims he is the last Messenger of God to humanity and the last prophet in a line which included Abraham, Noah, Moses and Jesus.

MOSQUE The place of worship and prayer. Also called 'Masjid'.

MUSLIM The name given to the followers of the religion of Islam.

PAGAN A person who does not believe in one God, but instead believes in many gods.

PBUH An abbreviation of "praise be unto him/ her". In Islam, it is often placed after the name of prophets as a sign of respect and honour. Sometimes the letters SAW are used instead. They stand for Sallal-lahu 'alayhi wa-alihi wa-sallam in Arabic, and mean 'Blessings and peace of God be with him and his household'.

PILGRIMAGE *See* Hajj

PROPHET A person who delivers a message from God to humanity. Muslims believe there were many prophets, including Abraham, Moses and Jesus, but that Mohammed (pbuh) was the last.

QUIYAM One of the positions used during daily prayer. It involves standing straight up with your hands at your sides. Say, "God hears those who praise him. Oh God, all praise be to you, O God greater than everything else."

QUR'AN The infallible holy book of Islam. It contains the word of God in its original form and without any modifications.

RAK'AH One unit of prayer. Each rak'ah involves several different positions and prayers. During daily prayers, Muslims may perform several rak'ah.

RUKU One of the positions used during daily prayers. Bend forward until the palms rest on the knees and the body forms a right angle with the straight legs. Women keep their arms close to their sides, but men keep them apart. Say "Glory be to God the great, and praise to him." Repeat this three times.

SALAH A word meaning prayer. It refers to the five daily prayers which are one of the five pillars of Islam.

SALAM An Arabic word which means 'peace'. It is also the name of one of the positions used in daily prayers and is said at the end of daily prayers, and is often heard in the Arabic phrase "Salaam Aleikum" (peace be on you), which is a common greeting between Muslims.

SEERAH An account of the life and accomplishments of the prophet Mohammed (pbuh).

SHAHADA The Muslim declaration of faith.

SHARI'AH *See* Islamic Law

SOHAR The meal eaten before dawn during the month of Ramadan. No food is allowed between sunrise and sunset.

SUJUD A position used during daily prayer. Prostrate yourself by kneeling, with your forehead, nose, hands, knees and toes all on the ground. Repeat "Glory be to my Lord, the Most High. God is greater than everything else," three times.

SUNNAH An account of the way prophet Mohammed (pbuh) conducted his life. It is meant to serve as an example for Muslims to follow.

SURAH One of the 114 chapters of the Qur'an.

TAKBIR The beginning of each daily prayer. Takbir is when a person faces Mecca and makes a clear decision to shut out the world to concentrate only on God.

TARAWEEH Special evening prayers performed during Ramadan. During each night's prayer, one juz (one-thirtieth) of the Qur'an is recited, so that by the end of the month the entire Qur'an is read out loud. The taraweeh is often recited by people who have memorised the entire Qur'an.

UMMAH The worldwide community of Muslims. It refers to all the Muslims in the world.

WUDU Special washing, or purification which is performed before offering daily prayers.

ZAKAH Also called almsgiving. This is one of the five pillars of Islam. Each person should give a certain part of their savings, usually one-fortieth (after expenses) to the poor and needy.

Index

Curriculum Visions

Curriculum Visions is a registered trademark of Atlantic Europe Publishing Company Ltd.

Atlantic Europe Publishing

Dedicated Web Site
There's more about other great Curriculum Visions packs and a wealth of supporting information available at our dedicated web site:

www.CurriculumVisions.com

First published in 2005 by
Atlantic Europe Publishing Company Ltd
Copyright © 2005
Atlantic Europe Publishing Company Ltd

Authors
Brian Knapp, BSc, PhD, and
Lisa Magloff, MA

Religious Adviser
Imam Kazi Abdul Kadir
MA Islamic theology, philosophy and law

Art Director
Duncan McCrae, BSc

Senior Designer
Adele Humphries, BA

Acknowledgements
The publishers would like to thank Imam Kazi Abdul Kadir and the London Islamic Cultural Society Mosque for their kind and generous assistance.

Photographs
The Earthscape Editions photolibrary, except 22–23 *Getty Images*.

Illustration
David Woodroffe

Designed and produced by
Earthscape Editions

Printed in China by
WKT Company Ltd

Muslim faith and practice
– *Curriculum Visions*
A CIP record for this book is
available from the British Library

Paperback ISBN 1 86214 468 0
Hardback ISBN 1 86214 469 9

This product is manufactured from sustainable managed forests. For every tree cut down at least one more is planted.